DON QUIXOTE
DE LA JOLLA

Eric Overmyer

BROADWAY PLAY PUBLISHING INC
New York
www.broadwayplaypublishing.com
info@broadwayplaypublishing.com

DON QUIXOTE DE LA JOLLA
© Copyright 1993 by Eric Overmyer

All rights reserved. This work is fully protected under the copyright laws of the United States of America. No part of this publication may be photocopied, reproduced, stored in a retrieval system, or transmitted, in any form or by any means, electronic, mechanical, recording, or otherwise, without the prior permission of the publisher. Additional copies of this play are available from the publisher.

Written permission is required for live performance of any sort. This includes readings, cuttings, scenes, and excerpts. For amateur and stock performances, please contact Broadway Play Publishing Inc. For all other rights please contact the author c/o B P P I.

Cover photo by Micha Langer

I S B N: 978-0-88145-109-2

First printing: July 1993
This printing: September 2016

Book design: Marie Donovan
Page make-up: Adobe Indesign
Typeface: Palatino

DON QUIXOTE DE LA JOLLA premiered at the La Jolla Playhouse (Des McAnuff, Artistic Director; Alan Levey, Managing Director; and Robert Blacker, Associate Director/Dramaturge). The first performance was on 7 August 1990, featuring the following cast and creative contributors:

DON QUIXOTE	Geoff Hoyle
THE BAND	Gina Leishman
SANCHO PANZA	Robert Dorfman
DULCINEA	Ellen Mcelduff
A BOY	Jonah Hoyle

Created in collaboration with Robert Dorfman, Geoff Hoyle, Gina Leishman, Ellen McElduff, and Stan Wojewodski, Jr.

Director	Stan Wojewodski, Jr
Set design	Neil Patel
Costume design	Christine Dougherty
Sound design	James LeBrecht
Lighting design	Stephen Strawbridge
Dramaturge	James Magruder
Stage manager	Michael B. Paul
Original music & arrangements	Gina Leishman

CHARACTERS

DON
SANCHO
DULCINEA
THE BAND—*a musician*
BOY

Author's note: The play was written for the La Jolla Playhouse. Specific La Jolla/San Diego references can be changed to fit the locale—DON QUIXOTE DE SEATTLE, DON QUIXOTE DE ARIZONA, DON QUIXOTE DE BILOXI...

This play is for Geoff Hoyle, Robert Dorfman, and Ellen McElduff, on whom, and for whom, it was written. They contributed much to the text besides their splendidly hilarious performances. And for Stan Wojewodski and Jim Magruder, in whose company I spent many happy dramaturgical hours on the deck of the Del Mar Il Fornaio, arguing the fine points of various gags over cappuccino. All of the above deserve credit as coauthors. And finally, this play is also for Des McAnuff, who brought us all together. Some fun.
—E O

(Music)

(The actor playing DON *skids on, dressed in period costume. Looks at audience.)*

DON: Yikes. Am I late? Sorry. We're still waiting for The Sancho. Or so I'm told. *(Looks at Swatch)* Anyway, on with the show. The show must go on, and all that. I'll tell you another show business adage, flip side of the show must go on: ten-thirty always comes. No matter how wonderful this time we have together is, no matter how exquisite, it's finite. Ten-thirty always comes. Don't be alarmed, you'll be long gone before ten-thirty. Ten-thirty's left over from the good old well-made never-come-again O'Neill three-act sawdust-on-the-barroom-floor father was a cheapskate sister was a doxy mother was a morphine fiend days. We won't see their like again. More's the pity. *(Checks his Swatch again)* And I couldn't possibly natter and vamp like this until ten-thirty, it's out of the question. Especially after what happened last night. Dunno how they managed last night. Dunno how they managed to keep it out of the papers. Well. So. How to begin. How to begin. While waiting for The Sancho. He's on his way, so I'm told. *(He rushes off. He rushes back on a moment later with a stack of stuff, including armor and helmet and various weapons.)* Whilst waiting for The Sancho. Something to pass the time. Of course, it would have passed in any case. Ladies and gentlemen—Quixote lazzi!

*(*DON *does some Quixote lazzi. Time passes. The actor playing* SANCHO *enters, dressed in street clothes, watches.)*

SANCHO: Wow.

(DON *stops and turns.*)

DON: Buenos días. At last.

SANCHO: I'm impressed. What do you call that?

DON: Quixote lazzi!

SANCHO: Lazzi?

DON: Classic comic archetypal character kinetics.

SANCHO: Gags. Bits.

DON: Gags?

SANCHO: Business. Schtik.

DON: Schtik.

SANCHO: It's very good.

DON: Thank you.

SANCHO: No, really. It's got style, it's got grace, it's got savoir-faire, it's got bouff.

DON: Bouff?

SANCHO: Absolutely. Tons of bouff. It's loaded with bouff.

DON: Are you The Sancho?

SANCHO: Well, I ain't the Donald.

DON: No, no, I'm the Donald. Er, I mean the Don.

SANCHO: You think that's too inside? Too New York?

DON: What? The Donald?

SANCHO: Yeah.

DON: Maybe.

SANCHO: I thought it was rather good, myself. Good retort.

DON: I thought you were supposed to be fat.

SANCHO: Excuse me?

DON: Chubby. Pudgy. Pear-shaped. Corpulent. Shaped like a sugar bowl. A walking cruller. Human brioche. Little fatso. Sancho. Sancho Panza, the Pillsbury Doughboy. Plump plum pudding of a fellow. Stuffed with proverbs, and all that.

SANCHO: I've been working out.

DON: Oh.

SANCHO: One-on-one weight training and complex carbohydrates. Listen, Don. May I call you Don?

DON: I don't see why not.

SANCHO: Don—

DON: And I shall call you Sancho.

SANCHO: *(Correcting him)* Sahncho.

DON: That's what I said. Sancho. Sancho Panza.

SANCHO: *(Correcting him)* Sahncho Pahnza.

DON: Sancho Panza. Sancho Panza. That's what I said. What's the problem.

SANCHO: Jeez. Nobody said anything about a Brit. A Tea Bag playing the Don.

DON: A what?

SANCHO: First Andrew Lloyd Webber—

DON: Well, I certainly didn't order up a midget shrimp to play my faithful squire Sancho Panza—

SANCHO: Midget shrimp is a redundancy. Unlike jumbo shrimp, which is an oxymoron. Like floating anchor. Guest host. British musical comedy.

(DON *and* SANCHO *do comparing heights lazzi.*)

DON: Least you could have done—as an erstwhile professional—was check downstairs with Costumes, get yourself a little padding. Nice fat suit. Eh?

SANCHO: Don't be ridiculous. I just got a hundred and fifty-dollar haircut. I'm not wearing a fat suit.

DON: Well. Can't be helped, I suppose. Just have to make the best of it, won't we? Just remember— ten-thirty always comes.

SANCHO: What does that mean, ten-thirty always comes?

DON: It's an adage. From the Golden Age.

SANCHO: Of Spain?

DON: Of The Show Business.

SANCHO: The Show Business?

DON: The Theatre. Before your time. When all the world was a stage, and Sir Ralph, Sir John, Sir Larry, Sir Alec, Sir Paul, and Sir Tyrone ruled it. Now, they were knights errant! We won't soon see their like again.

SANCHO: Yeah? Well what about Sir Marlon, Sir Jack, Sir Al, Sir Bobby, Sir Dustin, and Sir the Other Bobby? What about Sir Meryl? What about them?

DON: Movie actors.

SANCHO: Oh boy.

DON: It's hardly the same thing, is it? Weren't you in *Ishtar*?

SANCHO: No, but I've done two episodes of *The Equalizer*.

DON: Are you ready?

SANCHO: Yeah, but, uh, listen, Don. May I call you Don? Don, I'm uh, I'm not quite off book.

DON: I beg your pardon.

SANCHO: I don't have the lines down yet, okay?

DON: Unbelievable.

SANCHO: Hey. Don. Give me a break. Pretty short notice.

DON: Well, that's all right then, can't be helped, have to make the best of it. We'll improvise. I do most of the talking anyway.

SANCHO: I noticed.

DON: Just jump in when I stop.

SANCHO: With both feet.

DON: Doesn't know his lines. Won't wear a nice fat suit. Well, what do they expect? Get what you pay for. When the artistic director begged me to come down to the Playhouse to do Don Quixote, I told them to hire understudies. I warned them. Would they listen? Noooooo. They're so bloody cheap here, and then when the solids hit the fan, and the paddle disappears up the proverbial, they find out soon enough that every warm body worth a toss is either N I, not interested, N A, not available, O O T, out of town, or N O O T, not out of town in a million years. So what do you end up with? B L T. Bloody Local Talent.

SANCHO: *(To audience)* So what am I? C L? Chopped Liver? *(To* DON*)* I'll have you know I work a lot. In New York.

DON: New York. New York. Am I supposed to be struck speechless?

SANCHO: From your mouth to God's ears.

DON: I'm not impressed by the mere mention of New York.

SANCHO: Sure.

DON: New York does not impress me. I've played New York. Most provincial place in the country.

SANCHO: Bombed, eh? They hated you, right? You stunk up the joint.

DON: I don't feel the need to be validated in New York.

SANCHO: Sure. They all say that. Tell me you're not hoping that this is gonna come in.

DON: Absolutely not.

SANCHO: Right.

DON: New York is just another place to play, that's why I'm in La Jolla. In a supportive creative environment far from the corruptions of commercial theatre. That's why non-profit was invented.

SANCHO: Tell me another one.

DON: But my passion is my work! Commercial success would be merely frosting on the cake—

SANCHO: Sour cream on the bowl of borscht—

DON: Peach fuzz on the lip of prosperity. Now, you have read the book? The book. The novel. Oh, Sancho? Sancho?

(Pause. SANCHO looks at his feet.)

SANCHO: Can we talk?

DON: I don't bloody believe this.

(SANCHO brandishes the Smollett translation; it's huge.)

SANCHO: It's big. It's so big. It's a big book.

DON: Sancho, you have to have read the book. It's de rigueur.

SANCHO: It's heavy. I've got tennis elbow. I get migraines.

DON: We can't go anywhere if you haven't read the book.

SANCHO: I tried. But I got distracted by the dirty part.

DON: Dirty part? What dirty part?

(DON rushes to SANCHO, and they open the book.)

DON: I don't remember any dirty part.

SANCHO: First thing. Opening number. Page 31.

(The book falls open to a well-thumbed page 31.)

SANCHO: Right out of the gate. I got so excited, I sprained my thumb. I had to put the book down. It's way too heavy to hold in one hand. See?

(SANCHO tries to hold book in one hand, can't. Gives it to DON, who tries it too, unsuccessfully.)

DON: Where's the dirty part?

SANCHO: Right here.

DON: *(Reads)* "Accordingly, his armor being scoured, his steed accommodated with a name, his beaver fitted to his headpiece—" *(Pause)* I don't think it means that.

SANCHO: Don. You don't think beaver fitted to his headpiece means—beaver fitted to his headpiece?

DON: Well, yes, of course, beaver fitted to his headpiece means beaver fitted to his headpiece, but it doesn't mean—beaver fitted to his headpiece.

SANCHO: Then what does it mean?

DON: I dunno. But I don't think it means what you think you think it means.

SANCHO: Beaver.

DON: Beaver.

SANCHO: I think it does. I think it means beaver. Beaver, beaver, beaver. Beaver.

DON: Shut up. This is where a dramaturge would come in handy. They're like cops. Never a dramaturge around when you need one.

SANCHO: I mean, what else could beaver mean?

DON: I dunno, could be an animal.

SANCHO: On his head? Come on, Don.

DON: It's a problem passage.

SANCHO: It's a dirty passage.

DON: Got any Liquid Paper on you?

SANCHO: Oh, sure.

(DON *hands* SANCHO *some Liquid Paper.*)

DON: Better white out that beaver. Don't wanna get the Playhouse in hot water with the N E A, er, Spanish Inquisition.

(SANCHO *whites out beaver passage.*)

SANCHO: Goodbye, fair beaver. Adieu, sweet beaver. Okay. Done.

(SANCHO *hands book to* DON.)

DON: Whew. Now that we're expurgated, let us proceed. Hasn't read the book, doesn't know the lines, won't wear a nice fat suit, can't be helped, make the best of it, ten-thirty always comes. We'll carry this gallant tome with us on our travels, the Smollett translation, and read from it as the need arises. Selected bowdlerized passages. Now, I'll slip into my armor, and you carry the Smollett.

SANCHO: *(Whining)* It's so heavy.

(DON *hands the book to* SANCHO.)

DON: Come on. Read the rest of it. After the problem passage.

SANCHO: *(Reads)* "Accordingly his armor being scoured, his steed accommodated with a name—" *(Tries to make out what's under the white out)* something about a beaver— *(Reads)* "He reflected that nothing else was wanting, but a lady to inspire him with love; for a knight errant without a mistress would be like a tree destitute of leaves and fruit, or a body without a soul."

(Closes book) Or a fish without a bicycle. In other words, *cherchez la femme.*

DON: 'Twas ever thus. When was t'wasn't? 'Twas always *cherchez la femme.* Let us *vamanos!*

*(*DON *starts to get himself into armor and D Q getup.* SANCHO *hefts the Smollett.)*

SANCHO: Do I really have to carry the Smollett all night?

DON: You're the squire.

SANCHO: Even the curtain call?

DON: Yes.

SANCHO: It's so heavy.

DON: Quit whining and get into character.

SANCHO: I am in character. This is my character.

DON: 'Tis a noble quest upon which I and thou, Sancho, are engagest.

SANCHO: Engagest? Engagest? Look, Don, may I call you Don? Don, I'm sorry I didn't read the book, okay? I only found out about this *verkokte* job last night. I get home from the Gotham Bar and Grill three or four Harvey Wallbangers to the better—it's after midnight, there's a message from my agent, he says can you be in La Jolla tomorrow, I call him back, I say tomorrow are you kidding what does it pay, he says, eh, it's regional theatre but at least it's favored nations—it is favored nations, isn't it?

DON: *(Looking guilty)* Of course. 'Course it is.

SANCHO: What are you making?

DON: Same as you. Everybody makes the same. That's what favored nations means. Sancho.

SANCHO: What are you making? Come on, you can tell me. You can tell me, Don. I'm your squire. You can tell me. Come on, how much?

DON: Let's go. Allons! Vamanos!

(DON *whistles, and a bicycle rolls out of the wings.*)

DON: Aha! My faithful steed—Rozinante!

SANCHO: What about perks? What kind of perks are you getting? Come on, Don, I know you're getting perks. You're the Don, after all. The eponymous character. This is my first time at the Playhouse. I'm just the second banana. I mean, it's not called Sancho Panza de la Jolla, I know that. I can live with that, I wasn't born yesterday, I know how the business works.

DON: A car.

SANCHO: A car?

DON: A sub-compact.

SANCHO: A car! I knew it! A car! There is no such thing as favored nations. It's a myth! An Equity myth! A sub-compact, this is a deal breaker. I'm gonna go call my agent right now.

DON: Call him after the show. Saddle up, and let's move 'em out.

SANCHO: I suppose you have a jacuzzi, too. Well, you can do lazzi in your jacuzzi till the cows come home as far as I'm concerned. You should see where they put the peons. I mean, the freeway off-ramp runs right over my bedroom! What am I saying? It runs right through my bedroom! I-5 runs through my bedroom, I am not exaggerating! This is why I hate to work out of town!

(DON *mounts his bicycle.* SANCHO *finds a phone.*)

DON: I am ready to sally forth!

SANCHO: So sally, already. *(Into phone)* Phil, Tuesday, 8:15, Dorfman, La Jolla. *(Hangs up)*

DON: Walk this way. *(He rides off.)*

SANCHO: Walk this way? That is so old. And it doesn't even make any sense. You're riding a bike.

DON: You walk this way. And it's not a bicicleta, it is a noble steed, my own Rozinante! And you are my faithful squire, Sancho bleeding Panza.

SANCHO: *(Correcting him)* Sahncho bleeding Pahnza. *(Looks at cover of Smollett)* And it looks to me like I'm entitled to some locomotion of my own. A little burro or something.

(A smaller bike with burro ears wobbles out of the wings. SANCHO *catches it.)*

SANCHO: Love the ears.

(Checks seat. It's sticky.)

SANCHO: What is this? It's sticky. *(Feels it)* It's blood.

DON: It's not blood. It's stage blood.

*(*DON *hurriedly wipes blood off seat, then mounts Rozinante.* SANCHO *gets on his burro, pedals after* DON. *They go in circles.)*

SANCHO: I'm sorry I didn't read the book okay? I thought I'd read it on the plane, but there was a movie. By remarkable coincidence it was *Man of La Mancha*. Amazing. I know the stage play by heart but I've never seen the film before. It's not bad. Peter O'Toole, just great, Sophia Loren, can she make a peasant blouse stand up and bark or what, I'm telling you, a balcony you could do Shakespeare from. I don't know if Peter O'Toole did all his own singing. I think maybe they dubbed his high notes. Do you know?

DON: Do I know what?

SANCHO: If they dubbed Peter O'Toole in the movie.

DON: Of course they did.

SANCHO: They did?

DON: They dubbed him Knight of the Woeful Countenance.

SANCHO: Not Don Quixote. Peter O'Toole, did they dub Peter O'Toole—

DON: Well, they should have done. Dubbed him Sir Peter. Wonderful actor. But, it's all political, isn't it? Who your chums are, that sort of thing. He's had perhaps a bit too much fun in his life to be dubbed and knighted

(DON *rides off.* SANCHO *opens Smollett and reads.*)

SANCHO: *(Reads)* "The preparations being made, he could no longer resist the desire of executing his desire; reflecting with impatience, on the injury his delay occasioned in the world, where there was abundance of grievances to be redressed, wrongs to be rectified, errors amended, abuses to be reformed, and doubts to be removed; he therefore one morning in the scorching month of July, put on his armor, mounted Rozinante, buckled his ill-contrived helmet, braced his target, seized his lance, and through the back-door of his yard, sallied into the fields in a rapture of joy, occasioned by this easy and successful beginning of his admirable undertaking."

(*Sound of a crash offstage.* SANCHO *closes the Smollett, rides off. Music.*)

(*The actress playing* DULCINEA *enters, dressed as Marilyn Monroe in* Some Like It Hot, *carrying a ukelele. She sings and plays a song:* Running Wild. *She finishes. Exits.*)

(DON *wobbles on, looks after* DULCINEA.)

DON: Un apparition! My Dulcinea! Wellspring of my imagination, sacred lady of my soul.

(DULCINEA *and* SANCHO *tango across the stage—he dressed like a Spanish lounge lizard.* DON *watches them, in disbelief. They exit, dancing.*)

DON: I'll have the little bustard's guts for garters. I'll have the little bugger's head on a pike.

(SANCHO *enters, back in his street clothes, puffing, pushing his bike.*)

SANCHO: Sorry. You lost me on that last turn.

DON: I didn't know you could dance.

SANCHO: I've had a few lessons. It's on my résumé. Under special skills.

DON: That was quite the tango.

SANCHO: What?

DON: Quite the danse intime, with the lady of my heart, my muse, my flame, my Dulcinea

SANCHO: Don. May I call you Don? Don, I think you should take a pill, you're hallucinating, pal—

DON: Don't play the innocent, it doesn't become you. Where'd you learn to dip and sway like that? *Tango Argentina*?

SANCHO: I think you'd better chill before you freak, Don.

DON: Nasty, filthy, foreign dance. Next time I know you'll be dancing the Lambada!

SANCHO: The Lambada!

(DON *cuffs* SANCHO.)

DON: The forbidden dance!

SANCHO: The Lambada's not so bad, but it's really just the Hustle with a Brazilian twist. I much prefer a nice tango, myself.

DON: You're not Argentinean, are you?

SANCHO: Don't be ridiculous.

DON: *(German accent)* My father vas a Peruvian Indian, my mother vas a Peruvian Indian, und I am a Peruvian Indian. *(Own voice)* You know what an Argentinean is, don't you? An Italian who speaks Spanish and likes to think he's French. I guess we kicked your ass in the Falklands, didn't we? Eh? Guess Maggie Thatcher showed you what for, eh? *(As Maggie Thatcher)* "Let me reiterate, as I have said not once, but over and over and over again, the possibility that we would ever return the Falklands to the mainland is a possibility of a remotest possibility."

SANCHO: *(Correcting him)* Las Malvinas.

DON: What?

SANCHO: It's not the Falklands, it's Las Malvinas. And that was a disgraceful colonial adventure.

DON: You are Argentine.

SANCHO: Will you stop? I'm from Brooklyn.

DON: What about Grenada, then? Eh?

SANCHO: Grenada's in Spain. *(Correcting him)* Grenahda. The spice island. That was different. That was a movie. *Heartbreak Ridge*. Sir Clint.

DON: Oh, yeah, pull the other one, why don't you, it's got bells on it. What about Panama?

SANCHO: Hey, whatever works, right? I mean, we bagged the Big Pineapple, didn't we? El Grande Cara de Piña.

DON: What are you going to do with Noriega now that you've got him?

SANCHO: Make him a talk show host. How should I know? What do I look like, the State Department? Why is it whenever I meet a Brit, first thing they do is go off on American foreign policy? Am I responsible? Do I look like Henry Kissinger? *(As Henry Kissinger)* "Dis ends my hope for world domination." *(Own voice)* I'm an actor. But nooooo. Why'd you invade Panama? What do you think you're doing in Central America? Hands off Nicaragua. When are you going to pull the Cruise missiles out of Europe?

DON: Sancho—

SANCHO: And the Canucks are even worse. American cultural imperialism, McDonald's, Mickey Mouse, Madonna, yadyadyada. You know what Canada is? A country that could have had American know-how, French culture, and British government, and instead ended up with American culture, French government, and British know-how—

DON: I'm not sure I follow that. Could you repeat the punchline?

SANCHO: Hey, you missed it, tough. And it was easily as good as your Argentinean joke

DON: Sancho. Chill. Dude.

SANCHO: You're right. I'm fried. I'm toast. What a flight. It was packed. Five hours. Screaming babies, airline food, the worst. Coach of course. Try getting a first-class ducat out of a regional theatre. Good luck. And then the twelve-hour drive down from L A—

DON: I shall devise a tonic. An elixir. A remedy. *(He makes a tonic.)*

SANCHO: I could use a good stiff one right about now. By the way, did you know Noriega is a big big Don Quixote fan?

DON: No, really? General Noriega?

SANCHO: It's true. Huge fan. His favorite novel. After *Pride and Prejudice*.

DON: I didn't know that.

SANCHO: It's a little-known fact. You oughta send him an autographed glossy.

DON: Philistine.

SANCHO: *(Correcting him)* Philisteen. I went to school with Phyllis Stein.

DON: You never answered my question.

SANCHO: About Noriega?

DON: How you happened to be dancing the tango with my beloved Dulcinea?

SANCHO: What? The blonde bombshell?

DON: The flame of my innermost heart. My soul's delight and inspiration. Dulcinea.

SANCHO: That wasn't Dulcinea.

DON: That was Dulcinea! Dulcinea, queen of my inclinations!

SANCHO: To each his own, Don. But I think you got a bad case of the pedestal, pal. It's not healthy—for you or for her.

DON: You do not know Dulcinea.

SANCHO: I grant you. But I do know that blonde. Carmen. We worked together in Cleveland.

DON: Carmen? CLEVELAND?

SANCHO: Great Lakes Shake. We did *Funny Thing*. Terrific production. Well, say no more.

DON: I think I am in great need of succor—

SANCHO: Who isn't?

DON: Behold! My elixir! Balsam! *(He holds up his potion.)*

SANCHO: Balsam? What is that? Some kind of local tequila?

DON: It is a remedy. It salves the wounds of knight errantry and soothes the soul! This balm can heal a man though he be cleaved in two pieces.

(DON drinks, hands it to SANCHO.)

DON: I devised it myself, from an old medieval recipe.

SANCHO: Well, as long as it's from an *old* medieval recipe.

(SANCHO drinks too. Turns green, starts to vomit, rushes off. DON smirks, superior. Then he breaks out in a cold sweat. Starts to puke. Boy, is he sick. Does extended puking lazzi. Collapses. Recovers, gets to his feet. Smacks his lips)

DON: Ah! That really hits the spot! I'm myself again. Don Quixote de la Mancha.

(Music)

DON: What is a knight errant?

(DON quotes from Smollet:)

DON: "A knight errant is a scientist. He must know the law both of distributive and commutative justice. He ought to be a physician and botanist. He ought to be an astrologer, to distinguish by the stars the time of night. And besides being adorned with all the theological and cardinal virtues, he must know how to swim like an herring. He must preserve his fealty to God and his mistress; he must be chaste in thought, decent in speech, liberal in action, valiant in exploits, patient in toil, charitable with the needy; and finally, an asserter of truth, even though the defense of it should cost him his life. I am Don Quixote de la Mancha, redresser of grievances, righter of wrongs, protector of damsels, terror of giants, and the thunderbolt of war!"

(DULCINEA *walks across the stage, dressed like Marilyn Monroe in* The Seven Year Itch. *She stops over a vent, her dress flies up, she pushes it down, looks over her shoulder at* DON, *gives him a wink, and exits. He mounts Rozinante and sails out after her.* DULCINEA *immediately re-enters from another direction with a couple of cans of Tecate on a tray, as* SANCHO *enters simultaneously, now dressed in a* SANCHO *costume.*)

DULCINEA: *Hola*, Pancho. *Cómo va?*

SANCHO: Garbo speaks.

DULCINEA: How 'bout a cerveza?

SANCHO: Tecate, my favorite. *Una cerveza, por favor.*

(DULCINEA *pops the cans, hands one to* SANCHO.)

SANCHO: Gotta get the taste of that balsam out of my mouth. That is some elixir, that balsam. Nasty stuff.

DULCINEA: You drank the balsam? You're never supposed to drink the balsam.

SANCHO: Now you tell me.

DULCINEA: I thought everyone knew better than to drink Don's balsam. He makes it himself.

SANCHO: Now you tell me. *L'chaim.*

DULCINEA: *Salud*.

(DULCINEA *and* SANCHO *toast and drink.*)

SANCHO: You got a lime? A sliced lime would be nice.

DULCINEA: Sorry. Fresh out.

SANCHO: So how's it been doing this Don Quixote project?

DULCINEA: Well, it beats *Under The Yum Yum Tree* at the East Jesusville Dinner Theatre.

SANCHO: What about Don?

DULCINEA: Don't get me started. He's been after me to play all these other parts, quick changes, crone noses, facial hair.

SANCHO: Facial hair?

DULCINEA: He wants me to wear a moustache and play his mother.

SANCHO: Duenna costumes.

DULCINEA: Black muslin for days. I didn't come here to be unattractive, I came here to play Dulcinea. Look at this.

(A black shroud, head-to-toe duenna costume appears.)

DULCINEA: And it's not even cut on the bias.

SANCHO: Mercy.

DULCINEA: Tell you the truth, Pancho, I thought I was coming to do the musical, honest to God, they said do you play the market, I said no, the ukelele, they said great, I get here I find out he wants to do the book. I mean, the whole thing, both parts.

SANCHO: He wants to do the whole book, the whole enchilada?

DULCINEA: You know what happens in the book?

SANCHO: You tell me, I haven't finished.

DULCINEA: Nothing.

SANCHO: Nothing?

DULCINEA: Nothing. A big fat zero. Nada.

SANCHO: Nothing? Come on, Dulcy, it's a big book. It's big. Something must happen.

DULCINEA: I'm telling you, Pancho, nothing. I don't even appear. He thinks about me for a thousand pages.

SANCHO: Oh, I get it. Nothing happens to you.

DULCINEA: That's what I mean. I'm his muse. Lemme tell you, Pancho, that's tough to play. What's my action? What's my obstacle? What's my super-objective?

SANCHO: Sancho.

DULCINEA: I beg your pardon?

SANCHO: You've been calling me Pancho. My character's name is Sancho.

DULCINEA: I thought it was Pancho. Pancho Sanchez.

SANCHO: Sancho Panchez. Sancho Pancho. Sancho Panza.

DULCINEA: All this time I thought it was Pancho Sanchez.

SANCHO: Nope. That is incorrect.

DULCINEA: I've been laboring under a misapprehension.

SANCHO: I should say so.

DULCINEA: I always do that. I call chimichangas chichimingas.

SANCHO: Maybe you're dysxelsic, dysexlic, sexdyclic—

DULCINEA: The other Panchos never said anything.

SANCHO: Maybe the other Panchos were too polite. Say, how many other Panchos, uh, Sanchos, have there been?

DULCINEA: Scads.

SANCHO: What happened to them?

DULCINEA: They didn't work out. Of course, after what happened last night—

SANCHO: What did happen last night?

DULCINEA: Didn't they tell you?

SANCHO: No, they just offered me the job.

DULCINEA: And you took it. You should have called me, Bobby.

SANCHO: Is there something I should know about this engagement?

DULCINEA: Well, for starters, look at my contract.

(DULCINEA *pulls out contract.* SANCHO *reads it.*)

SANCHO: Babadababadaba, babadababadaba, boiler plate, boiler plate, agent bullshit, babadababadaba, uh-oh. Dulcinea, and—

(*Ominous music*)

SANCHO: As cast.

DULCINEA: I'm not playing the fat housekeeper, I don't care what anybody says.

SANCHO: The Don's got a thing for fat suits, doesn't he?

DULCINEA: It's a fetish. Fat suits. Facial hair. Audience participation.

(SANCHO *pulls out his Liquid Paper.*)

SANCHO: I never go anywhere without my Liquid Paper. (*Whites out As Cast*) Earlier this evening I whited out a dangerous beaver. There you are, my dear. Now you are contractually amended. No mas as cast.

DULCINEA: *Muchas gracias,* Pancho.

SANCHO: *No hay de que.*

DULCINEA: You're so sweet. I thought you were sweet in Cleveland, too.

SANCHO: I thought you were the bee's knees.

DULCINEA: You did?

SANCHO: Absolutely. The cat's pajamas. I had an enormous crush on you. But you were dating that Hollywood hack.

DULCINEA: Oh, him. He's history. He's a residual.

(*Music.* SANCHO *starts to move.*)

SANCHO: Whenever I hear that crazy beat. I just can't stop dancing. I can't even eat my lunch in peace.

(DULCINEA *and* SANCHO *merengue. Boy, are they good.*)

DULCINEA: Oh, Pancho.

SANCHO: *Ay, chica!*

(DULCINEA *and* SANCHO *merengue off. A loud crash is heard offstage. Terrible sounds.* DON *wobbles on, beaten to a bloody pulp.*)

DON: That looked suspiciously like a merengue.

(SANCHO *enters, once more in street clothes, carrying the* Smollett, D Q Cliff Notes, *and some take-out Chinese.*)

SANCHO: Don, where have you been? I've been looking all over for you. I've been worried sick.

DON: You've been doing the merengue with the light of my life, Dulcinea.

SANCHO: Don, don't start with me, okay?

DON: You're Dominican, aren't you?

SANCHO: Will you get out of here?

DON: Next thing I know, you'll be dancing the Lambada!

SANCHO: Lambada!

(DON *cuffs* SANCHO.)

DON: The forbidden dance!

SANCHO: The Lambada's not so bad. I much prefer a nice merengue myself.

DON: I could have used your company and assistance, old friend. I've been beaten and left near death by a band of bloody-minded Yanguesian carriers, evil, vicious, nasty web-footed blackguards of the first order.

SANCHO: Sounds like fun. Sorry I missed it. Besides, I'm a pacifist. You know what they say. Whether the baseball hits the plate glass window, or the plate glass window hits the baseball, it's going to be bad for the window.

DON: Proverb. I detest proverbs. But at least you're getting into character.

SANCHO: I am in character. This is my character.

DON: I abhor proverbs.

SANCHO: Well, as my grandmother always said, sometimes you eat the gefilte fish, and sometimes the gefilte fish eats you. Wait, that's not right.

DON: *(Notices Cliff Notes in SANCHO's hands)* What is that?

SANCHO: What? This? Kung pao chicken.

DON: That.

SANCHO: *Cliff Notes.*

DON: *Cliff Notes?*

SANCHO: You know. Crib sheets. *Don Quixote Cliff Notes.* Your key to the classics.

DON: Philistine.

SANCHO: For a good time call Phyllis Stein, we always used to say. You had to be there. Although you, Don, no hard feelings, I don't know if you woulda fit in. Listen, Don, I'm just trying to catch up here.

DON: Doesn't know his lines, hasn't read the book, won't wear a nice fat suit, has recourse to vulgar crib sheets, well, can't be helped, make the most of it. Ten-thirty always comes, eh?

SANCHO: I'm sure it does. So, listen, Don, what about the windmills. I hope you haven't done the windmill gag yet, have you? 'Cause I don't wanna miss that, I wanna be there for the windmill lazzi, I've been looking forward.

DON: If you are referring to the adventure in which I encounter thirty or forty giants, engage them in single-handed combat—

SANCHO: With my assistance—

DON: —Only to find the giants transformed at the last moment by my arch enemy, the evil Enchanter, into windmills—that event has not yet occurred.

SANCHO: That's the one.

DON: I'm saving it for later.

SANCHO: I couldn't agree with you more, Don. Good narrative strategy. I know this Cervantes cat was an Oscar winner during the silent era but according to these Cliffies, Vhe does the windmill lazzi just after the main titles, practically, and it's straight downhill from there for another nine hundred pages. I mean, this windmill tilting is obviously an act three predenouement sort of thing and you don't wanna shoot your wad while the people are still sitting down with their popcorn, it's a story point, if you know what I mean. Now, the way I figure it, we'll give Miguel a "from an idea by" credit, he should be happy with that, he's dead, and you and I will share the "screenplay adapted from another medium by" billing, I've got a call into Phil as we speak, and I wouldn't dream of not being there with you by your side when the windmill thing comes down, Don, baby. Now. According to the Cliffies, and I could be wrong because I haven't read the book, so correct me if I'm talking through my sombrero, Don, according to the Cliffies, you shmooze me with islands, and governorships, and more moolah than I've ever known heretofore, if I'll just come along and schlepp your bags.

DON: I persuade you to come on a great adventure.

SANCHO: You persuade me to leave my wife and kids. Right here, wait a minute— *(Consults the Smollett)* Way back on page sixty. And I quote: *(Reads)* "The knight said so much, used so many arguments to persuade, and promised him such mountains of wealth, that this poor simpleton deserted his wife and children." *(Closes book)*

DON: You give up the humdrum and domestic for a life of adventure and knight errantry.

SANCHO: I don't think the Mrs is gonna see it quite that way. That stuff doesn't really wash anymore, does it? I mean, this wandering son of a sailor idea is pretty tired, and so are buddy pictures. And let's face it, Don, this is a buddy picture, and it's a tired genre. It's a buddy picture, it's a road picture, it's a male bonding thing, and it needs a spin.

DON: Isn't that a bit reductive?

SANCHO: Maybe it is. All I'm saying, Sancho's backstory could be a little more sympathetic, don't you think? Maybe we could make him a divorced but caring father who's frustrated by his limited visiting privileges.

DON: Absolutely not. We stick to the spirit, if not the letter, of the book.

SANCHO: I think you're gonna have to make some concessions to three hundred and fifty years of progress.

(DON looks at audience.)

DON: You call this progress?

SANCHO: You may have a point.

DON: I'll take la Mancha over La Jolla any day.

SANCHO: That's 'cause you're a registered Democrat.

DON: I'm not even a citizen.

SANCHO: Do you have your green card?

DON: *(Looks guilty)* 'Course I do.

(BOY enters. Tree and moon appear.)

BOY: I have a message for you, Sir.

DON: Yes?

BOY: Mister Godot says to tell you he cannot come today.

(Pause. DON considers this astounding news.)

DON: Tell him—

BOY: Yes?

DON: Tell him—

BOY: Yes, Sir?

DON: You say Mr. Godot can't make it today?

BOY: No, Sir. But he will surely come tomorrow.

DON: Tell him—

BOY: Yes, Sir?

DON: Tell him we'll be here.

BOY: Yes, Sir. *(He exits.)*

(DON and SANCHO look at each other. DON pages through the Smollett.)

DON: Godot? I don't recall any Mister Godot.

SANCHO: Contract. Where's my contract? I haven't seen a contract, yet.

DON: *(Paging through)* There's no Godot here.

(THE BAND *whistles. Holds up* SANCHO's *contract. Many names have been crossed out and the name of the actor playing* SANCHO *has been added in big letters.* THE BAND *tosses the contract to* SANCHO.*)*

DON: They've got it all wrong. There's no Godot in Don Quixote—

SANCHO: *(Catches contract)* Thanks. *(Examines it)* It's sticky. Blood! There's blood on my contract!

DON: It's not blood.

(DON *takes contract from* SANCHO, *wipes it off, hands it back.)*

DON: It's stage blood.

SANCHO: Really?

DON: Why would I lie about a thing like that?

(SANCHO *looks through his contract.)*

SANCHO: There's nothing in here about Samuel Beckett. And what are these other crossed-out Sanchos? I better call Phil.

DON: Call him at the interval.

SANCHO: What'll we do 'til then?

DON: Let's go.

(Pause. DON *and* SANCHO *do not move. They're frozen: existential paralysis.)*

DON: They do not move.

SANCHO: I noticed. I noticed.

DON: This is worrisome.

SANCHO: No kidding.

DON: Man is born astride a grave. The light gleams an instant, and is gone. Something about forceps.

SANCHO: Don. You're scaring me, Don.

DON: Let's go.

(Pause. DON and SANCHO do not move.)

SANCHO: They do not move.

DON: This evening is unbearable.

SANCHO: Unendurable.

DON: It's awful. Worse than the Music Hall.

SANCHO: The Circus.

DON: The Pantomime.

SANCHO: The Circus.

DON: The Theatre.

SANCHO: The Circus. The Circus. Trust me on this. The Circus.

DON: This is exactly what I hate about modern life. Wouldn't you rather be tilting at windmills than waiting for Godot?

SANCHO: I grant you. This is not my favorite lazzi, this stasis lazzi. In fact, stasis lazzi is an oxymoron.

(Music. DULCINEA cha chas across the stage and disappears. DON is released.)

DON: Dulcinea! I am released from my enchantment!

(DON whistles, Rozinante appears, and he sails off after DULCINEA. She enters from another direction This releases SANCHO from his enchantment, and he joins her.)

DULCINEA: *Hola,* Pancho. *Como va?*

SANCHO: Better. I'm just getting over a touch of existential paralysis. But I'm feeling more myself. More chipper.

DULCINEA: I'm so glad to hear it.

SANCHO: But I gotta tell ya, Dulce, I'm kinda concerned. This play doesn't seem very—set—if you know what I mean.

DULCINEA: Every night is different.

SANCHO: Yeah? Sounds exciting. So, just what was different about, say, oh—last night's performance?

DULCINEA: I can't talk about that now.

SANCHO: Dulcy, baby, please, I'm begging you.

DULCINEA: Lemme put it this way, Pancho. A word to the wise. If you know what I mean.

SANCHO: I think I do.

DULCINEA: I can say no more.

SANCHO: Please, say no more.

DULCINEA: You gotta be prepared if you wanna improvise.

SANCHO: I understand, believe me.

DULCINEA: I can say no more.

SANCHO: Please, say no more.

DULCINEA: Lemme put it this way, Pancho. Watch your back.

SANCHO: Watch my back? This is why I hate to work out of town.

DULCINEA: I can say no more.

SANCHO: Please, say no more.

DULCINEA: Ten-thirty always comes.

SANCHO: One can always hope.

DULCINEA: If you're lucky. I can say no more.

SANCHO: Please! Say no more!

DULCINEA: I was just trying to be helpful. An ounce of prevention—

SANCHO: I know. And you strike me as a girl who knows her way around a proverb.

DULCINEA: I love proverbs.

SANCHO: I got some proverbs of my own I'd like to share with you. At a later date.

DULCINEA: Oooh, say no more, please.

SANCHO: When I'm not worried about certain things.

DULCINEA: What things?

SANCHO: Oh, certain minor details. Like not knowing my lines. Like not knowing what play I'm in. Like not knowing—

(He pulls out his contract.)

SANCHO: —whose blood is on my contract. WHOSE BLOOD IS THIS, ANYWAY?

DULCINEA: Oh, that blood. That's stage blood.

SANCHO: Stage blood.

DULCINEA: Huh-huh. Stage blood. Hershey's syrup, red dye number two, some chopped gauze—

SANCHO: What's the chopped gauze for?

DULCINEA: Texture.

SANCHO: Texture. Of course.

(Music)

DULCINEA: Music.

SANCHO: Latin music.

DULCINEA: Lubricious Latin music.

SANCHO: Whenever I hear that crazy beat

DULCINEA: Don't tell me—

SANCHO: I can't even eat my lunch in peace

DULCINEA: I know what you mean.

SANCHO: I just can't stop dancing!

DULCINEA: *Pobrecito!*

SANCHO: Lambada!

(They Lambada. Boy, are they good. They Lambada out. DON and Rozinante stagger on. Blood streaming; one of DON's ears hanging by a thread.)

DON: That lubricious Latin dance looks suspiciously like the Lambada!

(SANCHO's head pokes up out of trap.)

SANCHO: Lambada!

(DON drags SANCHO bodily out of the trap. SANCHO's got the balsam.)

DON: The forbidden dance!

(DON cuffs SANCHO. DON's ear comes off in his hand.)

DON: Ooo, I hate it when that happens. *(He reattaches his ear.)*

SANCHO: This reattaching severed ear lazzi is very good, I love this.

DON: Ah! There we are!

(SANCHO gestures. DON feels his ear. It's upside down. He straightens it.)

DON: There we go.

SANCHO: How'd you lose your ear?

DON: Doing battle with the evil Yanguesian carriers.

SANCHO: Those web-footed guys again? Don't they ever give up?

DON: I could have used your assistance, son Sancho.

SANCHO: I know, I know, I shoulda been there.

DON: Instead you were dancing a lubricious Latin dance—

SANCHO: Don't say it

DON: With my beloved Dulcinea—

SANCHO: I'm begging you—

DON: The Lambada!

SANCHO: Lambada!

(DON cuffs SANCHO.)

DON: The forbidden dance!

SANCHO: I asked you not to say it.

DON: My ear aches. I am in great need of succor.

SANCHO: Uh-oh.

DON: Hand me my elixir, my tonic, my remedy, my—

SANCHO: Don't say it—

DON: My balsam!

(DON grabs balsam. SANCHO cuffs DON, grabs balsam back.)

SANCHO: Balsam! Cookie Tossing! The Forbidden Lazzi!

(SANCHO throws balsam away. DON fumes.)

DON: Hasn't read the book, doesn't know his lines, won't wear a nice fat suit, dances lubricious Latin dances with the leading lady every chance he gets, destroys the props, won't join in any reindeer games. We're hopelessly out of order here, and we'll never catch up.

SANCHO: What do you suggest?

DON: Gather your things, ready your burro, gloss the Smollett, and—let's go!

(DON and SANCHO both start to move, freeze for a long moment, then break, pointing and laughing at one another.)

DON/SANCHO: Hey? Eh? Hey? Eh? *(They do not move!)* Hey? Hey?

SANCHO: I had you goin', didn't I? Hey? Eh?

DON: Admit it, you were terrified.

SANCHO: I did experience a brief jolt of pure existential adrenaline I confess. You're very good at that. Have you ever considered a career as a living mannequin?

DON: After tonight, a career as a living mannequin would be the impossible dream.

SANCHO: Dare to be great, Don.

DON: And so I shall, son Sancho.

(DON produces a letter.)

DON: Take this letter to my beloved Dulcinea.

(DON hands the letter to SANCHO, who reads it all the way through.)

SANCHO: *(Jack Benny)* Oh. Oh, Don.

DON: Yes?

SANCHO: *(Jack Benny)* It's in Spanish.

DON: Find pen and paper, I shall translate.

(SANCHO looks for pen and paper but can't find them. DON quotes from the Smollett:)

DON: "Sovereign and sublime princess, he who is wounded by the edge of absence, and whose heart is stuck full of the darts of affliction, wishes thee that health which he is not doomed to enjoy. I can ill support the misery I bear. If it be thy will to succor me—"

SANCHO: Succor. Don't tell me Carmen does balsam, too. This company is like a collection of weird bulemics.

DON: "For I am thy slave; if not, the end of my life will satisfy thy cruelty and my desire. Thine 'til death, the Knight of the Rueful Countenance."

(SANCHO *finally borrows a pen from someone in the audience and writes down last line.*)

SANCHO: "Knight of the Rueful Countenance." Wow. Where do you get this stuff? Don, you are some epistolary stylist, I'm telling you.

DON: Do you think it's good?

SANCHO: Like everything you do, like every move you make, like every breath you take, like every cake you bake, it's loaded with bouff. A little long on the self-pity, but, I gotta say, overall, it works for me.

DON: Then get thee on thy burro, and to my lady Dulcinea.

SANCHO: One more thing. Isn't it supposed to be woeful? Woeful countenance?

DON: Rueful. Rueful countenance. Page 192. The Smollett. You can look it up.

(SANCHO *gets on his burro.*)

SANCHO: *(To* DON*)* Which way did she go? Which way did she go?

(DON *points.* SANCHO *sails off.*)

SANCHO: *(Offstage)* No brakes!

(*A scream. A crash.* DON *permits himself a smile. Comes downstage.*)

DON: *(To audience)* Now that we're alone, sans Sancho—what about some nice—AUDIENCE PARTICIPATION? *(He works the crowd.)* I am I, Don Quixote, the Lord of la Mancha. My destiny calls and I go. After spending the night at an inn, I sally forth, but refuse to pay the bill, because knights-errant don't have to pay, ever. Didn't know that, did you? It's a nice side benefit of the business, it is. Anyway, I sally forth, and what do I see, but a cloud of something nasty coming after me. A huge cloud of dust. And I figure it must be an army. In fact, it's so big, I figures it must be two armies! Now, what I don't know in my madness is that this cloud of dust is really a flock of sheep. In fact, it's really two flocks of sheep. Okay, now, we're going to divide the audience into two parts. Yes, that's right, you guessed it, you're going to be the sheep. Ready? Baaaaa.

(DON *gets first one side of the audience and then the other to baa and baa.* DULCINEA *comes in, takes a look at what* DON's *doing, shakes her head, and walks out. He doesn't notice her, so engrossed is he in shepherding his sheep. He's got them baaaing away.* SANCHO *enters, bloodied and beaten.* DON *stops mid-baaaing.)*

DON: *(To audience)* Hold that thought. *(Goes over to* SANCHO*)*

SANCHO: Sounds like it's going well.

DON: Very well. They're really a good group. What happened to you?

SANCHO: This and that. First, I discovered my burro has no brakes. And then I was set upon—

DON: Sat upon? Like a sofa?

SANCHO: No, no, set upon by ruffians, and beaten like a lutefisk—

DON: Lutefisk?

SANCHO: You know what I mean, beaten like a lutefisk from head to toe, within an inch of my life, by a gang of thugs and brigands.

DON: Evil Yanguesian carriers!

SANCHO: No, Don, your creditors. There were mugs there from Hotel Del, La Valencia, Cafe Pacifica. You're running up tabs all over town. Skipping out on checks. You're a deadbeat! A schnorrer! A mooch! Your picture's on every cash register from Chula Vista to El Cajón. They roughed me up pretty good. They were big. They were big guys. Took my wallet, I gotta call Phil, get him to cancel my credit cards—

DON: You know what you should have said? Stopped them in their tracks.

SANCHO: No, what?

DON: You should have said, "You are a saucy publican, and a blockhead to boot." What about the letter?

SANCHO: Letter? What letter?

DON: My eloquent epistle to my enchanting Dulcinea.

SANCHO: Oh, that letter. I still got it. Not to worry, I guarded it with my life. I wasn't gonna let those hooligans from Cafe Pacifica get this letter, no way. What kind of squire do you think I am, anyway?

DON: Did you deliver it?

SANCHO: Like I said, I was on my way when I was waylaid by highwaymen. But I'll get on it right away.

DON: Immediately.

SANCHO: If not sooner. *(He starts out.)*

DON: Oh, Sancho.

SANCHO: Yes, Don.

DON: Just deliver the letter. The sooner the better. And only the letter.

SANCHO: Sure, the letter, deliver it, the sooner the better, what else?

DON: If I discover you've been doing anything like—

SANCHO: Oh, no—

DON: Dancing—

SANCHO: Don't say it—

DON: A lubricious Latin dance—

SANCHO: Oh, God, here it comes—

DON: With my beloved Dulcinea—

SANCHO: I asked him not to say it—

DON: For instance, the Lambada!

SANCHO: Lambada!

DON: The forbidden dance!

(DON *cuffs* SANCHO, *as usual, but this time* SANCHO *protects himself with a World War I doughboy helmet.* DON *hits his hand on the helmet with a terrific thunk and screams in pain. He does a broken hand lazzi, which* SANCHO *adores.*)

SANCHO: This broken hand lazzi is terrific. I love this. It's so real. You could almost believe the man is really in pain.

DON: Why'd you do that?

SANCHO: Don, I remember from the musical, which I know by heart, that you need a nice Golden Helmet of Mambrino. So I was down in the village, I picked up a little doughboy number, let's see how this works—

(SANCHO *puts the helmet on* DON.)

SANCHO: Oh, that's nice. You're lovely, absolutely lovely. You look just like the F T D logo. Wingèd Mercury. You just need some little Vulcan ears—

DON: Will you get going? And take the duenna with you.

(SANCHO *picks up duenna costume.*)

SANCHO: Love that hat. There can be no hat like thee. *(He goes out.)*

DON: Typical. Can't do anything right. Now, you lot were going— *(Goes to one side)* Baaa baaa baaa—and you lot— *(Goes to one side)* Were going baaa baaa baaa—

(DON gets them going, too)

DON: And I bravely wade amongst you single-handed, and lay waste to the pack of you— *(He wades into the audience.)* Ignoring the cries of astonished shepherds— "Hey, what you fink you're doing? Leave my bleeding sheeps alone, you great dingleberry—" *(Flails about wildly)* And I flail about wildly and I hit my hand— *(Hits his previously injured hand— Excruciating pain)* And it hurts like hell. *(He screams silently, dancing up and down the aisle in pain. Staggers back onstage, where he recovers himself, somewhat. Searches in vain for his balsam)* And I look around for my succor, my elixir, my bloody balsam, which my bleeding squire, Sancho bleeding Panza, has confiscated in a rare fit of comic good taste— *(Beat)* When suddenly— *(Beat)* I AM ATTACKED BY A WILD CAT!

(A piece of fur falls on DON's face. He struggles with it, wildly. Ferocious wild cat lazzi. Eventually it takes him through a closed door, which he flattens, and offstage.)

(DULCINEA and SANCHO appear. SANCHO shows DULCINEA the letter. All that is written on it is—)

DULCINEA: *(Reads)* The Knight of the Rueful Countenance.

SANCHO: Guess I musta missed his opening remarks.

DULCINEA: Isn't it supposed to be woeful? Woeful countenance?

SANCHO: We talked about that. He prefers the Smollett. I hope I can remember how it went. I wish I'd paid closer attention.

DULCINEA: Don't sweat the details, Pancho. Be mas mucho! Improvise!

SANCHO: I will! *(He clears his throat.)* I'll skip the part about his gall bladder, it's disgusting. "O most fair enemy! O gorgeous foe! O cruel Virgin!"

DULCINEA: Oh, please.

SANCHO: "I am suffering. I am suffering, a lot! Woe is me. Because you are such a beautiful, lovely, exquisite, excellent, exotic damsel—"

DULCINEA: Same old stuff. *Mucho mas picante,* Pancho!

SANCHO: *Mas macho,* eh? O most scrumptious, mouth-watering, scintillating, intoxicating, creamy delicious, delectable, absolutely yummy, tiramisu of my soul—

DULCINEA: *Mas mejor!*

SANCHO: Creme brulee of a paloma pie!

(DULCINEA and SANCHO clinch.)

DULCINEA: Is this you talking, Pancho, or Don?

SANCHO: What do you think?

DULCINEA: I thought you were shy.

SANCHO: Nothing ventured, nothing gained.

DULCINEA: Oh, Pancho. A proverb! I love proverbs!

SANCHO: I got a million of 'em.

DULCINEA: I want to hear them all.

(Music. DULCINEA *and* SANCHO *start to dance. To waltz)*

SANCHO: You can lead a horse to water, but a pencil must be lead. A closed mouth gathers no foot. In the land of the blind, the one-eyed man is king. Make yourself honey, and the flies will be all over you like a cheap suit. Who can hedge in the cuckoo? Keep the pressure on. Bread is relief from all griefs. Sleep is the remedy for all our waking miseries. The only thing wrong with sleep is that it looks a lot like death. Death is that country from which no traveler returns. You've never really known a man until you've seen him die. One shouldn't talk of a rope in the house of a hanged man. Never pay retail. From your mouth to God's ears. Sleep faster, we need the pillows. Sol, meet me halfway, buy a ticket. Stick your hand in a blender, it's quicker. Let every man put his hand on his heart, and not set himself up to call right wrong or wrong right, for we are all as God made us, and some a good deal worse. Every night is different. Ten-thirty always comes. The show must go on. There are no people like show people, they smile when they are low. There are no small parts, only small paychecks. There is no such thing as net. You haveta be prepared if you wanna improvise. It's a fine line between homage and parody. No, that's not right. It's a fine line between homage and plagiarism. That's man all over for you, blaming on his shoes the faults of his feet. One of the thieves was hanged. What goes around comes around. Another happy day. It's not the heat it's the humidity. You can run, but you can't hide. Something about forceps. Qua qua qua qua qua qua—

(DULCINEA *and* SANCHO *waltz out. Just as* DON *staggers in, as usual, bruised and bloody, and carrying the subdued wild cat, and wearing part of Rozinante.*)

(*He stares after them.*)

DON: Was that my beloved Dulcinea? Wellspring of my imagination. Sacred lady of my soul. Queen of my inclinations. Flame of my innermost heart. Dancing the Tennessee Waltz? With my faithful squire Sancho Panza? Looked like it. Well, at least they weren't doing the—

(SANCHO, *disguised in the duenna schmatte, appears.*)

SANCHO: *(Falsetto)* Lambada?

DON: Lambada!

SANCHO: *(Whacks DON with his fan)* The forbidden dance!

(DON *staggers, but recovers.*)

DON: Art thou my beloved Dulcinea? At last? Who deigns to speak with me?

SANCHO: *(Re: cat fur)* Is that a dead beaver around your neck, big fella, or are you just happy to see me?

DON: It is the corpse of a wild cat I have vanquished, and present to you, my lady, as a token of my fealty.

SANCHO: Keep your cat corpse for some other girl, and let's Lambada!

DON: Lambada!

SANCHO: *(Whacks him with his fan)* The forbidden dance!

(Music)

(They Lambada. Boy, are they good. They Lambada all over the stage.)

(Just as they Lambada past the phone, it rings. SANCHO *can't help himself, he answers it.* SANCHO's *veil slips)*

SANCHO: Hola, qué tal? Oh, Phil— *(To* DON*)* It's my agent. *(To phone)* Listen, can I call you back? I'm in the middle of something, here—

(DON *steps back, suspicious.*)

SANCHO: I know, I know, I know, the time difference is murder. I need to talk to you, too, but I'm right in the middle of a hot date. Right. Love to Adele.

(SANCHO *hangs up, sees* DON *looking at him.*)

DON: Just as I suspected!

SANCHO: Uh, oh.

(DON *rushes to* SANCHO, *rips off his veil and mantilla.* SANCHO *stands revealed. He cowers.* DON *gathers himself.*)

DON: Thou art more lovely than I remembered.

SANCHO: Thank you. *(Double take)* What?

DON: More radiant than the morning sun.

(DON *kneels before* SANCHO, *and kisses his hem.*)

DON: More beautiful than all the stars in heaven's firmament. More succulent than a bingèd cherry.

SANCHO: Don. You're scaring me, Don.

(SANCHO *tears himself free, rushes off.* DON *throws his cat around his neck, gets on his piece of Rozinante, and sails out after him. Terrible crash offstage.* SANCHO *re-enters a moment later, still in duenna duds,* DULCINEA *in tow.*)

SANCHO: He's flipped. He thinks I'm you. It was just a gag. I thought he'd get a kick out of it. You know the Brits, two drinks and out come the dresses.

DULCINEA: He's been playing this part too long.

SANCHO: You gotta talk to him. Tell him you're you.

DULCINEA: I make it a policy never to talk to Don, onstage or off.

SANCHO: Make an exception. I gotta dodge Don until I can doff these duenna duds.

DULCINEA: I don't know, Pancho. I hate to break my vow. Even for you.

SANCHO: Please, I'm begging you. Uh-oh, here he comes. *(Looks around)* Let's hide in the band!

(DULCINEA *and* SANCHO *climb up on the bandstand, grab instruments.* DON *enters, looks around, calling.*)

DON: Dulcinea? Dulcinea? Dulcinea?

(DON *sees them.* DULCINEA, SANCHO, *and* THE BAND *are all wearing big handlebar, Zapata moustaches. Attached to Groucho glasses, i.e., gaucho glasses.)*

DON: Ah ha!

*(*DON *strides up to them. They cringe.)*

DON: A band of trolling mariachis! *(He picks up a violin.)* Mind if I sit in? I won't take no for an answer.

(They play and sing a mariachi number.)

ALL: Tortilla, taco, quesadilla, salsa.

SANCHO & THE BAND:	DULCINEA:
Chichimanga	Chichimanga

ALL: Enchiladas verdes, tostadas, flautas, margaritas, flan, cafe con leche, la cuenta por favor!

(During the number, SANCHO *manages to wiggle out of his duenna costume.)*

(They finish. Big finish.)

DON: That was wonderful. Thank you. *(Scrutinizes* SANCHO*)* Is that you, Sancho?

SANCHO: Yes. Yes, it is.

DON: I didn't recognize you. Have you lost weight?

SANCHO: I grew a moustache.

DON: Ah, that's it. *(He turns to* DULCINEA.*)* And you, Señora.

DULCINEA: *Si, Señor?*

DON: You, too, remind me of someone—

SANCHO: *(Hopefully)* Dulcinea?

DON: Don't be ridiculous, Sancho. My beloved Dulcinea does not not sport a Zapata moustache. *(To* DULCINEA*)* Although, it is very becoming on you, my dear.

DULCINEA: *Muchas gracias, Señor.*

DON: *(To* THE BAND*)* And you, my dear, you too are *muy linda.*

THE BAND: Thank you.

DON: *(To* DULCINEA*)* No, my dear, you remind me of someone else. Someone nearer and dearer, yet farther away. Someone from my past. I can't quite remember who. Well, no matter. *(He doffs his cat to* THE BAND *and* DULCINEA.*)* Ladies. Come with me, son Sancho.

*(*DON *takes* SANCHO *by the arm and leads him from the bandstand. The ladies remove their moustaches and* DULCINEA *slips away.)*

DON: The women of this village are very attractive. But we must find my beloved Dulcinea. Did you read her my letter?

SANCHO: I paraphrased.

DON: I see. And how did she respond?

SANCHO: Favorably. Very favorably.

DON: Excellent. The time is propitious to press my suit.

SANCHO: I'd be happy to run it down to the dry cleaners for you.

DON: Wonderful. You go that way—

*(*DON *points.* SANCHO *looks.)*

DON: And I'll go this way.

*(*DON *sails out.* SANCHO *looks back, and* DON *is gone.)*

SANCHO: Well, he'll be back. Where does he have to go?

*(*DULCINEA *enters, steaming. Literally. Steam rising off her clothes.)*

DON: I hope you're happy.

SANCHO: What? What? What did I do? You look like you're steamed about something. What's the matter?

DULCINEA: You made me break two of my favorite vows. You made me talk to Don.

SANCHO: Only a few words in Spanish. That's not so bad.

DULCINEA: And you made me wear facial hair onstage!

(DULCINEA *starts to sob.* SANCHO *comforts her.*)

SANCHO: Listen, calm down.

DULCINEA: My career is over!

SANCHO: Will you stop? You look very fetching in gaucho glasses.

DULCINEA: I do?

SANCHO: Yes! And we have other things to worry about.

DULCINEA: We sure do. *(She pulls out a tabloid.)* Will you look at this headline?

SANCHO: *(Reads)* "Plastic Surgeon's Goof Gives Man Pelican Bill."

(DULCINEA *grabs tabloid back, and reads correct headline.*)

DULCINEA: "Woman claims she got pregnant doing the Lambada."

SANCHO: Dulce, a big I Doubt It. Really.

DULCINEA: Really?

SANCHO: Really. Never happened. Trust me. Calm down. Okay?

DULCINEA: Okay.

SANCHO: Now. We just gotta hang on until ten-thirty finally comes. Don is gone. Totally. He's in a world of his own. There is no area code for his number.

DULCINEA: Whatever you say, Pancho.

SANCHO: Just humor him, do whatever he tells you to do, and keep a straight face.

(DON *enters with two fat suits—his and hers.*)

DON: Ah! There you are! My faithful squire, Sancho Panza!

(DON *gives* SANCHO *a fat suit*)

DON: And my fat housekeeper!

(*Gives* DULCINEA *a fat suit*)

DON: For you, my dear. Now, don we all our gay apparel, and we'll begin.

(DULCINEA *and* SANCHO *get into their fat suits.* DON *goes offstage.*)

DULCINEA: This makes three. Three of my favorite vows.

(SANCHO *finds something on his fat suit.*)

SANCHO: What is this? It's sticky. It's blood! There's blood on my fat suit! Whose fat suit is this, anyway?

(DON *rushes on with a large trunk.*)

DON: Prepare yourselves for the play!

(DON *opens his trunk and gives* SANCHO *and* DULCINEA *costumes.*)

(*The trunk becomes a puppet stage. A sign hung above it says:* The Adventures of Don Quixote de La Jolla.)

(*Rain effect.* DON *looks to heaven.*)

DON: Is it raining? 'Tis a typhoon brewing. We must take refuge, son Sancho.

(DON *stops in front of the puppet stage.*)

DON: Ah! Sancho! Here's a castle! With entertainment! *(To* DULCINEA*)* A room for two, my good woman. And what time does the play begin?

DULCINEA: I think it's already in progress, Señor.

DON: No matter. I know this theatrical by heart!

*(*DON *sits himself down before the stage, waits expectantly.* DULCINEA *gestures to* SANCHO, *who reluctantly follows her behind the stage.)*

DULCINEA: *(Pulling on her hand puppet)* This makes four. Four of my favorite vows.

SANCHO: Which vow is this?

DULCINEA: The working with puppets vow.

SANCHO: Puppets aren't so bad. I once had a gig doing voices for an animated movie. *The Gummi Bears Christmas Special.*

DON: *(Clapping hands)* I recognize this scene. This is where Don Quixote and Sancho take refuge from the rain in an inn full of evil, web-footed Yanguesian carriers, and watch a puppet play.

DULCINEA: That's the one, your grace.

SANCHO: *(To* DULCINEA*)* You know how this goes?

DULCINEA: Relax, Pancho. Just improvise like a puppet.

SANCHO: Puppet improvisation, sounds like an oxymoron to me.

*(*SANCHO *manipulates two puppets, a* DON *puppet and a* SANCHO *puppet.* DULCINEA *manipulates a* DULCINEA *puppet.* DON *claps his hands when the puppets appear.)*

DON: Here come the mummers!

SANCHO: *(*SANCHO *puppet)* Hola! Cómo va!

DULCINEA: *(*DULCINEA *puppet)* Welcome, Señors, to the puppet show!

SANCHO: (SANCHO *puppet*) What's playing, Señors?

DULCINEA: (DULCINEA *puppet*) This is the scene where Don Quixote and Pancho Sanchez come to this inn, and watch a puppet play about Don Quixote and Pancho Sanchez who come to this inn to watch a puppet play.

SANCHO: What is this? Pirandello? If our puppets are here to watch a puppet play shouldn't our puppets have puppets?

DULCINEA: Work with me here, Pancho. (DULCINEA *puppet*) Welcome to our show, Señors. So glad you could make it. Aren't you Don Quixote? And his faithful squire, Pancho Sanchez?

SANCHO: (SANCHO *puppet*) That's us! (DON *puppet*) I am I, Don Quixote. And thou art my beloved Dulcinea!

DULCINEA: (DULCINEA *puppet*) No, your grace, I'm merely your mistress of ceremonies. Me llamo Carmen.

SANCHO: (DON *puppet*) Thou art not a mistress of ceremonies, thou art my beloved Dulcinea, inkwell of my inquisitions, castanets of my Spanish soul! (*Other voice*) Down in front! Down in front! (DON *puppet*) Who said that? Who dared to speak to Don Quixote de la Mancha in such a tone of voice! (SANCHO *puppet*) Your grace, this tavern is full of those evil web-footed guys who are here to see the puppet show, too! (DON *puppet*) Yanguesian carriers? Here? They dare to darken this door? (SANCHO *puppet*) It's a very popular puppet play, your grace!

DULCINEA: Uh, Pancho, I wouldn't talk about the Yinyangian characters—

SANCHO: (SANCHO *puppet*) That's the ones, Señora! The place is crawling with them! Look!

(SANCHO *puts down his* SANCHO *puppet, and comes up with an evil web-footed Yanguesian carrier puppet.*)

SANCHO: *(Yanguesian puppet)* Like I said, pal, down in front!

(DULCINEA *is horrified.*)

DULCINEA: Oh, Pancho! Not the Yinyangian character puppet!

(SANCHO *examines Yanguesian puppet.*)

SANCHO: Radical feet, dude. *(He makes his Yanguesian puppet grab* DULCINEA *puppet. Yanguesian puppet)* Yo, Carmen! What time do you get off, doll? Lambada! *(He makes the puppets Lambada.)*

DON: The forbidden dance! Unhand my Dulcinea, you fiend! *(He draws his sword.)*

SANCHO: Uh-oh.

DULCINEA: He's got the vapors. Way to improv Pancho.

(DON *growls, waves his sword menacingly.*)

SANCHO: Don't panic, I'll think of something. *(He attacks Yanguesian puppet with* DON *puppet.* DON *puppet)* Take that! And that! And that, you web-footed fiend! *(*DON *puppet pulverizes Yanguesian puppet.* DON *puppet)* There! Vanquished! *(*DON *puppet—to* DON*)* I did it! I, Don Quixote de la Mancha! I slew the cursed web-foot! And now I can sit back—and relax—and enjoy the rest of the show. In my seat. And maybe I'll just check my sword—

(DON *is halfway persuaded back into his seat, when he changes his mind and switches his focus from the puppets to* SANCHO.)

DON: I know who thou art!

SANCHO: *(*DON *puppet)* I am you, Don Quixote, and I'm gonna watch this nice puppet show, and then I'm gonna go home and have some ice cream and turn on the tube, catch some of that quality British television, like Benny Hill—

DON: Thou art my arch enemy! The Evil Enchanter! Thou hast dared to turn me into a puppet! And where ist my faithful squire, Sancho Panza? What hast thou done with him, o Foul Enchanter?

SANCHO: I'm here! I'm here! Don! This is me! Sancho!

DON: And where is my beloved Dulcinea?

DULCINEA: *(Waving her puppet)* Here we are! Here we are!

DON: Thou art not Dulcinea! Thou art an actress! An impersonator! *(To* SANCHO*)* And thou art an actor! And a poor puppeteer!

(DON *charges them.* DULCINEA *and* SANCHO *flee.* DON *decapitates the puppets, and destroys the puppet stage. Runs amok. Runs off.* DULCINEA *and* SANCHO *return.)*

SANCHO: Is this what happened last night?

DULCINEA: This is worse. Much worse.

(DON *runs on.)*

DON: Michael, roll the film! *(He pulls down a movie screen. Goes behind a curtain.)*

SANCHO: Film? What? What is he doing?

(Film starts. It's a film of DON *riding Rozinante on the beach, doing battle with the Evil Enchanter, etc. Quixote lazzi.)*

DULCINEA: He's been making a film. He wants to direct.

SANCHO: Who doesn't?

DON: *(From behind curtain)* I smell a rat in my lady's credenza! *(He stabs through curtain. He charges back on stage. He sees them.)* Ah ha! There you are!

(DULCINEA *and* SANCHO *run off.* DON *starts after them, but his eye is finally caught by the film. He stands transfixed at his own image. Film ends. Lights up. He is stunned by what he's seen. He puts down his sword.)*

DON: That was awful. Dreadful. I'm so ashamed. And I thought I had talent. Who am I kidding? I'm a fraud! A charlatan! A poseur! *(He clutches his heart.)* I am with myself—as an artist—and a human being—disenchanted!

(DON flails about, clutches his heart, has a heart attack. Does heart attack lazzi. Lies still. SANCHO and DULCINEA come cautiously back on.)

SANCHO: Is this what happened last night?

DULCINEA: This is worse. Much worse. He looks kinda peaked. Do you think maybe he's muerto?

SANCHO: Nah. Impossible. He's just so good, that's all. It's easy to be fooled.

(DULCINEA and SANCHO get out of their fat suits as they go over to DON.)

SANCHO: *(Jack Benny)* Oh, oh, Don? *(As SANCHO)* Don?

DULCINEA: If Don dies onstage, is that an out? I better call my agent.

(DULCINEA hands SANCHO her fat suit, heads for exit.)

SANCHO: Hey, where're you going?

DULCINEA: Pancho. I'm not in this scene. This is the deathbed scene. It's just you and the fat housekeeper, and I'm not playing the fat housekeeper.

SANCHO: You're in this scene in the musical.

DULCINEA: This isn't the musical, amigo. This is where the blonde checks out, and the boys bond.

SANCHO: Dulce, it's not like that, trust me. Hang around.

DULCINEA: You made me break four of my favorite vows. I didn't come here to be unattractive. I came here to play Dulcinea. I may have been born yesterday, Pancho, but I've been up all night. *(She exits.)*

SANCHO: El Torito after the show?

(No answer. SANCHO *props* DON *up with fat suits. Talks in his ear.)*

SANCHO: I know you're in great need of succor, Don, but we're temporarily out of balsam, and you're gonna have to whip up a new batch. That sounds like a project, doesn't it? And Rozinante will be out of the shop in a couple of days, and before you know it you'll be back on the boards again. And you can show me how the windmill gag goes. I been looking forward.

(No response)

SANCHO: Don, this deathbed lazzi is terrific, but I think it's getting a little extended, if you know what I mean. Don, let's go. *(Beat)* They do not move. Yikes. Don, you're scaring me, Don.

(No response)

SANCHO: You know, Don, I was talking to the Artistic Director in the wings, during one of my offstage sallies, and he wants to do a project for me next season, not one of these Classics Illustrated numbers, but a musical revue. And I'm thinking, I could use a good second banana, if you're interested, and I have a call into Phil as we speak, if you need representation, I'd be happy to refer you, I think you could go either way, legit or musical, you're a major talent, c'mon, Don, you're dead, and we're dyin' out here, let's go.

*(*SANCHO *makes a move, freezes.)*

SANCHO: They do not move.

*(*DON*'s eyes flutter open.)*

SANCHO: No, they do! They do!

DON: What news of the Rialto, friend?

SANCHO: The news is, ten-thirty has come at last, just as you predicted.

DON: At last?

SANCHO: Absolutely! Hell, in New York, it's one-thirty in the morning, and we're at the Stage Door Deli, noshing on a nice turkey and chopped liver on rye, with pickles.

DON: Sounds revolting. Is that you, Sancho?

SANCHO: This is me, Don.

DON: I had a terrible dream. I dreamt that I was playing Don Quixote in La Jolla and my faithful squire Sancho Panza didn't know his lines.

SANCHO: Didn't know his lines? Ridiculous. Just an actor's anxiety dream. You know what they say—*la vida es sueño.*

DON: A proverb. I detest proverbs. But at least you're getting into character.

(DON *struggles to his feet.* SANCHO *helps him.*)

SANCHO: I am in character. This is my character.

DON: I am a very foolish old man—

SANCHO: You're not so old—

DON: I fear I am not in my right mind. Madness is a remote thing which can be attained with infinite slowness by those who have the patience. I am a sea gull. No, that's not right. I am a performance artist. I am a seagull, I am a performance artist. Ah, well. More of this anon, and now to bed.

SANCHO: That's it? We're done?

DON: Our revels now are ended.

SANCHO: No more lazzis? But we didn't do the windmills. We gotta do the windmills, Don.

Everybody's looking forward. You cannot do *Don Quixote* without which you do the windmills.

DON: Windmills tomorrow, tragicomedy tonight.

(Romantic rhythms. DULCINEA *enters, dressed in gold lamé Marilyn Monroe dress from* Gentlemen Prefer Blondes. *Phone rings. She to phone, answers it.)*

DULCINEA: *Hola, qué tal?* Oh, hi, Phil? Really? Sure, I can catch the red eye, no es problema. Billing? Just Carmen. No last name. Right. Like Charo. Uh-huh, okay. Listen, Phil, —can you have a car waiting? Lincoln stretch. White. Okay. See you on the set, sweetie. *(She blows a kiss into the phone, hangs up.)*

SANCHO: El Torito?

DULCINEA: I got a plane to catch, Pancho. Love makes time pass. Time makes love pass. *(She gives* SANCHO *a big wet one and exits.)*

SANCHO: It would have passed in any case. *(To* DON*)* So, Don, whaddya think? You game to give this another go tomorrow night?

DON: I don't know, Sancho. I was thinking, I may go back to the Bay Area, open up a nice little bicycle repair shop.

SANCHO: Don, Don, stick with me here a minute, Don. All I'm saying is, we got the makings of a terrific team here—

DON: We do?

SANCHO: Absolutely. Bud and Lou, Stan and Ollie, Kramden and Norton, Didi and Gogo, Winnie the Pooh and Piglet—

DON: Winnie the Pooh and Piglet?

*(*SANCHO *walks* DON *around in a circle.)*

SANCHO: Sure, when they're looking for the Woozle.

ACT THREE

DON: Look, there's two tracks—

SANCHO: Look, there's four tracks—

DON: Look, there's eight tracks—

SANCHO: Don't look back, something might be gaining on us—

DON: Satchel and Paige!

SANCHO: See? We're a duo.

DON: Well, in spite of not knowing your lines, not reading the book, having recourse to vulgar crib sheets—

SANCHO: Hey, I did wear a nice fat suit, whaddya want from me?

DON: This may work out.

SANCHO: We gotta remember to do the windmill gag tomorrow night.

DON: And the penance scene. Where you flog me.

SANCHO: I could get behind that.

THE BAND: And don't forget the weird ocarina bit— (*Plays a snatch of the theme from* The Good, The Bad, and the Ugly.)

SANCHO: And I got a few requests of my own. I wanna play my paper bag banjo, and sing a *Running Wild* duet with the new Dulcinea. And I wanna solo on *Don't Cry For Me Argentina*—

DON: You are Argentine, aren't you?

SANCHO: Don't start with me, Geoff, okay? May I call you Geoff?

DON: Certainly. And I shall call you Bobby.

SANCHO: What's Spanish for Geoff?

DON: El Jefe!

SANCHO: So listen, El Jefe, you're gonna haveta level with me about what happened last night and whose blood is all over everything.

DON: All in good time, Bobby. Tomorrow night. One more chance to get it right.

(SANCHO *picks up his burro and they start off.*)

SANCHO: That sounded like a proverb to me. For a guy who doesn't like proverbs—

DON: It's an adage. There's a difference.

SANCHO: From the Show Business, I suppose.

DON: Where else? From the Golden Age! Make a note, we must remember to do the ever-popular haggis-stuffed-with-mummer lazzi, where I pop out of a sheep stomach.

SANCHO: Sounds like fun.

DON: And the astral projection lazzi—and let us not forget the déjà vu all over again lazzi.

SANCHO: Oh, no, I draw the line at déjà vu all over again—

(DON *and* SANCHO *disappear down the vom.*)

END OF SHOW

www.ingramcontent.com/pod-product-compliance
Lightning Source LLC
Chambersburg PA
CBHW071757040426
42446CB00012B/2593